PHOTOSONATA

PHOTOSONATA

Martin J. Desht

[signature]
16 APRIL 2016

Foreword by Gerald Stern

FINE GRAIN BOOKS · SANTA FE

*For Susan
and for Jerry*

To Cath and to Chip

Acknowledgements

MANY HAVE GIVEN generous support and encouragement over the years. Among those I'm greatly indebted to for their critical insights and advice are Gerald Stern, Anne Marie Macari, Philip Levine, Robert A. Kavesh, Danielle Nisivoccia, Alan Trachtenberg, Henry Louis Gates, Jr., Alicia Suskin Ostriker, Barry Holstun Lopez, Rosalind Pace, Kenneth J. Endick, Cynthia Starr, MD, William A. Pencak, editor of *Pennsylvania History,* Lee Arnold and Matthew Lyons of the Historical Society of Pennsylvania, and Desmond Bell of Queen's University, Belfast. For their consistent kindness and encouragement, I wish to thank Robert J. Smith, Christa Hopf, Basha Zapatka, Michel Durand, Scott and Kristina Moore, Russell and Margaret Moser, Robert and Joan Fenton, Lee and Ann Heumiller, Richard Master, John F. Mitchell, MD, Edward J. Gillespie, William Kreitz, and William H. Fisk III and family.

For legal advice pertaining to photography, thanks are due to Joseph C. Hollywood, of Easton, Pa., and to John W. Caldwell, member, Philadelphia Volunteer Lawyers for the Arts.

I express a particular debt of gratitude to George T. Ridout, Sr. Without his knowledge, courage, guidance and friendship, my Philadelphia work would not have been possible.

To Diane Shaw, of Special Collections at Lafayette College, I offer many thanks for her early and continuous support of my work. I'm grateful also to Richard E. Sharpless, of Lafayette's History Department. His astute foresight and guidance were essential to my documentary work in Pennsylvania.

Gladys Miller-Rosenstein, of the Puffin Foundation, I thank again for her generous and continuous support since 1996. And I wish to thank The Virginia Center for the Creative Arts, in Amherst, Virginia, for offering space and time to conceive and organize portions of this book.

The gratitude I owe to my wife Susan Heumiller for her love, patience, and critical eye for detail, and to her late mother Charlotte Sonntag Heumiller Knapp, is immeasurable.

Contents

FOREWORD

DESHT HAS THE FINEST EYE FOR RUINS of any photographer whose work I have seen. He was lucky—or doomed—to grow up in the midst of the Pennsylvania Rust at its most glorious—and horrible—time. His photographs constitute a record—I would say *the* record of the end of an era. There's a touch of nostalgia about them but it's more that of a survivor rushing back into the fire for a last look before it's all gone. There's a touch of bitterness too but it's primarily a gorgeous memory of what we lost as a nation as well as what Desht personally lost, for he lived and worked there.

As for his poetry, for this book is photography *and* poetry, it treats the vision and the experience the very same way as do the photographs. "Because You Want To Love," for example, or "Crane Gang." Though words and images get the thing done somewhat differently. For my money, Desht is a very fine poet—and the poetry shows the same anger, stubbornness, bitterness, love and vision the photographs do. Martin is my friend and I'm proud, very proud, of this book.

GERALD STERN
Lambertville, New Jersey
September, 2014

Documentary: That's a sophisticated and misleading word. And not really clear ... The term should be documentary style ... You see, a document has use, whereas art is really useless. Walker Evans, 1971.

Photography is the art of writing with light. And at least since the eighteen-nineties documentary photography has been presented as a collection of images almost invariably with written texts to suggest interpretations of those images. Texts ranging from simple identifying titles to lengthy captions to entire books are meant to "give voice" to the otherwise silent images. In a sense they attempt to "proof" the images, to make them mean this instead of that—descriptive words used to confer idea or clear purpose to the ambiguous art of photography.

On the street I try for "straight photography," for less emotional tone and more neutrality, for more seeing rather than interpreting what's before the public eye. Yet the very ambiguity of writing with light seriously challenges this approach and gives rise to some persistent questions. How do I show fair objectivity in a subjectively perceived world? How do I convince the public of my thesis? (Document, from *docēre*, to teach.) Can I illuminate the narrative in light without resorting to the narrative in words? Can I make a series of images that both convey my ideas and speak truly for themselves? It is more than idle questioning because the answers betray my attitude and perception of the subject, my intention in pursuing it, the style and method of presenting it, and will inform my decision as to content, tone, and length of any text that will accompany the images.

Photographs without accompanying texts are often interpreted by understanding their social or historical contexts, or by assuming the implications of the immediate environment in which they are seen. It is well-known that a photograph pasted in a wedding album and later found stapled to a police file may suggest very different interpretations. An unattached image, that is, one without a text, is a moveable feast that shows its versatility and power to lead you to ponder and perhaps define its relationship exclusively to the world in which you found it. Unstaple the same photograph and let it be found taped inside a fallen soldier's helmet.

So pliable are lone photographic portraits that it is typical for a viewer to pose questions of Who are you? What do you mean? And, sometimes, in a curious reversal, one may sense a photograph's response of Who are you? and What do you mean?

If captions and context can lead to interpretation, it should be said that documentary photographs can conceal as much as they reveal, which often leads photographers to commence writing about their images, or to team up with writers. Jacob Riis spent years writing and staging slide shows for the propertied class. Lewis Hine broke new ground by pairing images with words to depict not just facts but what he called "human documents." Margaret Bourke-White shadowed Erskine Caldwell as they traveled the back roads of the Deep South. Dorothea Lange first teamed up with Paul Taylor, then married him. Evans joined Agee and let him do the writing, nearly five hundred pages worth. In *Les Américains*, Kerouac careened into Beat lyricism while Robert Frank wrote his blunt one-liner titles and little else. For my work, out of a spirit of independence and reflective questioning, almost from the beginning I have done my own writing.

To make a claim for truth and neutrality is a hazardous business of course, because for the documentary photographer it is the text or narration that is the trip-wire—the mix of words with images that can undo any careful documentarian. Polemics will be seen as an attempt to coerce viewers as to how they should perceive and react to the subject; whereas minimal narrative influence may be a gesture to allow viewers to arrive at their own conclusions. There is much fluid space between these two approaches, and Evans hints that for the conscientious documentarian, the way, or *documentary style,* is seldom clear and the footing always precarious.

Some years ago I made an effort to list the various relationships between image and text; to show how they react when they meet eye to eye on a page or on a gallery wall. Some of my findings are at the end of this book.

Photosonata is divided into two groups of photographs made in Pennsylvania at the end of the twentieth century: scenes of small industrial towns and workers followed by scenes of Philadelphia. The first group are accompanied by poems of remembrance. The second group by poems I regard as songs for a city. As do many books of photographs, *Photosonata* recalls a geography and a way of life; a past, because as music exists in the time of now, photography's realm, and its truth if any, is in the time of then.

Documentary work is a convergence of three points of view. These are the historical visual record, the social context of time and place, and the metaphorical record consisting of the visual and literary sensibility that one's knowledge and personality bring to the work. I generally agree that a photographer's attitudes and emotions should be at a remove from good documentary work. Conveying easy emotion or sentimentality isn't difficult, and work that relies heavily on this risks being light on intellect. Agree also that, one way or another, separating emotion and intellect is improbable, if not impossible.

The photographs in this book were obviously made for a documentary project, yet *Photosonata* is neither a documentary exhibit nor an ecphrastic work, that is, a book that employs creative writing to define or interpret the photographs. The practice of *photo-ecphrasis*, as I call it, where a poem's inspiration and subject are derived from a readily available photograph, is an art I leave to others. Here, no poem is matched with an image to "speak" for it, and their placement within the book is intuitive. It is my hope that the poems speak for themselves and reveal their own images.

This book is a record of my impressions and experiences working as a photographer in Pennsylvania. A partial record, of course, since my experiences and the acquaintances and friendships I made were beyond what any camera could record.

They were beyond words, too.

———

Interviewer: *Do you think today that art is something useful?*
Ingmar Bergman: *It has to be. And if it's not useful, we can go to hell.* (1970)

Note on the Photographs

FOR MUCH OF THE TWENTIETH CENTURY, the Keystone state was the most heavily and diversely industrialized enterprise in America. Pittsburgh was famous for its black sky and thirty miles of riverside steel mills. Philadelphia billed itself as "the workshop of the world." The Pennsylvania Railroad traversed half the country and the state's anthracite fueled the nation. By the century's last decades, as America's economy shifted from industrial manufacturing to service and information, both cities became notorious for urban decay and industrial abandonment.

The nineteen-eighties and nineties were difficult times for blue-collar workers. Industrial jobs and generations of industrial culture, of an American way of life, were vanishing before their eyes. Factory outlets replaced factory workers. Casinos replaced steel mills. Those who found post-industrial service jobs took home thinner paychecks. Some who did not re-train or find work re-acted and found something else, and in April, 1995, it was reported that Pennsylvania had more white-supremacists and neo-Nazi gangs than any other state in the nation.

Many of these photographs are from the exhibit FACES FROM AN AMERICAN DREAM. The exhibit's theme concerns how this economic transition re-defined American industrialism in rural communities, small factory towns, and in cities, particularly Philadelphia, and what it meant for skilled and unskilled workers in search of the American dream. The list of communities that suffered from de-industrialization is long and intense. But with its massive industry and workforce, its miles of factory-like brick row homes, only Philadelphia could claim to be "the workshop of the world."

Images for the exhibit were collected from 1989 to 2001 using 35mm and 6cm x 6cm medium format film cameras. Developing, printing, mounting and framing were done in my darkroom in Pennsylvania. Lafayette College's Williams Center for the Arts, in Easton, sponsored the first exhibit in January, 1992. FACES FROM AN AMERICAN DREAM has been on tour ever since, having traveled to New York University's Stern School of Business, Harvard University, Dartmouth College, United States Department of Labor, United States Senate, among many other venues.

The Eye sees more than the Heart knows. William Blake.

I

After Photographing
Adam Zagajewski

Now I read his name before a poem
and hear his voice just before I read it—
sputtered English mixed with broken Polish,
like my ancient mother Katrin Pavlik—

smiling, Kracόw lisp, knowing winter
stench and war, lines of spattered mules
and muddied poor trailing great carts
of rags. Dusk of boiled soup and bones.

Hunger night of wild kicking dreams—
Sea. Ship. A Bremen wave at last.
Then a port. A pier. A waiting Vincze Déšť.
A kiss. *Ameryka*.

II

CRANE GANG

WE GET TO IT by climbing sixty-two rungs on a ladder that's straight up and caged. The ingot mould stripper crane spans a pit sixteen feet deep and hardly groans when its gorilla arms cradle three hundred tons of steel as thick and obtuse as a Stonehenge lintel. Four of us. Motor Inspectors, Dept. 413. Beth-Steel Electrical Maintenance: Schleicher-123, Kastelnik-166, Fronheiser-232 and Desht-174. Danny and Rick up for a fuse check on a dead string of mercury vapors, thousand-watters that tint the skin blue, your lips the color of raw liver. And Fronny and the new-kid-Desht up for a hot coil on a chattering relay, then for lunch and a quick shut-eye nooner on the roof, our "Patio," a slim piece of grated catwalk between the baghouse dust collector and the rising stacks of E.F.M., Electric Furnace Melting. With a view. Where the smog christens the steeples of Lehigh University and swirls around the high-rise dorms before it drops like a yellow rag over East Third and Polk.

Fronny calls *This way, sweetie,* and steps across the crane trackway and I follow because I'm his Electrical Helper and still young and beautiful, he says. We monkey over the crane's cab and after he twists his shoulders and big ass through the empty window frame, I hand-off my pail and thermos then trapeze through the open space landing on the walk with a faint thump, still being light and lithe at a hundred sixteen pounds.

On the grate Fronny turns with a sour look. Then smiles, then coughs a wad and spits loud and wet. The gob slimes down the tarred corrugated, the thick silver trail glistening in the sun until it thins and stops just before reaching the sole of Joey Hausmann's shoe—"Little Joe," who's sleeping curled in a corner which happens to be Fronny's favorite perch for his noon crossword. Fronny drops his belt and settles himself against the struts of the 32 kv power line, a jagged march of high tensions that jump westward roof to roof as far as we can see. Doffs his hardhat and takes a pack of Winstons from the webbing. Rakes through his sweaty hair, looks to me putting a finger to his lips because everyone knows Hausmann wants to take hold of your elbow and ask what will save his leukemic kid from jumping off the Minsi Bridge to crash through the roof of No. 6 Machine Shop.

But of course only ever stares and never asks.

For the rats and red-eyed pigeons, Danny and Rick set out little packets wrapped in Easter purple and green, sprinkle the fine pellets along the crane trackway and into the hollows under the eaves. Sowing it like seeds over the cab's roof and the crane's walkways, throwing a handful under the relay boards. Lay a fresh coat over the coagulated puddle around the grease pump. Stardust, we call it, since even in what appears as total darkness the crystalline pellets seem to catch any lost ray of light and sparkle.

For Fronny and me, it's a sandwich with a foggy view of southside Bethlehem. The Windish priest on Daly Avenue sweeping maple blossoms off his steps with a wide push broom. The ore freight paralyzing traffic from East Third to Wyandott to the Hill-to-Hill bridge. The spectacle on the dorm balconies of the Lehigh girls tanning their oiled thighs from pizza to career. Mongrels and mutts chasing kids on tricycles. Pink sheets swaying on a clothesline.

Fronny relaxes against the cool struts, pitches the last of his sandwich into the billet scrap yard below. Reaches into his hat and starts a new chain. Slips the pencil from his ear, unrolls his *Globe-Times* and is gone. I finish a Butterscotch Krimpet and wash it with black coffee still warm from home. Save the Red Delicious for later. When the world's smoking all around you it's hard to quit. So I light up and study Hausmann, 413-212. Lately said to be Foreman, Looper material. Twelve years and not once caught napping in a cab or fuckin'-the-dog. Seems now Joe never eats.

When he rolls southward, his face beams serenely in the sunlight, the glow as if a mask over years of age and toil. I watch the rise and fall of his breath guttering out of his opened mouth, the plum-colored dust coating the pearls of his teeth.

At last the ore freight rocks and creaks past the boxy houses on Amplex Street. Cars on East Third start a crawl of beetles in a slow parade. Through a window a hand flips the Closed sign in Gert's Bar. McFadden blows the horn for a furnace pour. Fronny rolls his paper into a stiff tube and tucks it down his shirt. In ten minutes he'll be leaning over a hoist motor to block the limit switch and the tube will flatten soaked with sweat and stuck to his hairless chest. The ink will smudge and he'll be pissed. Later we'll sneak into Mac's office and Fronny'll swipe his copy and a handful of Velvet No. 2s. Some fresh Ray-O-Vac D cells if someone's been careless and he doesn't have time to pick a lock. *Never know what'll pop open with a cute little hacksaw blade.*

We rise, strap our belts. I grab up and swing through the window frame and land squarely on the cab's roof with cat-like precision. Fronny follows, squeezing his army-green bulk through the frame and asking me what the hell's a four letter word for song.

——

Schleicher was one of the most competent crane electricians at the Bethlehem plant. Kastelnik worked middles and nights and took day classes in computer languages. Robert Fronheiser was killed while performing a crane hoist inspection. Desht worked middles and nights and took day classes in literature.

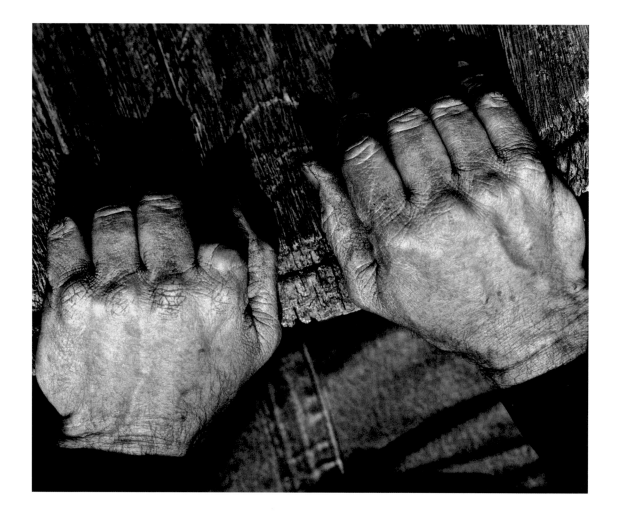

III

BECAUSE YOU WANT TO LOVE

for Gerald Stern

You've known for the last forty miles
on Interstate 95 that by the time you get
to Aramingo Avenue you'll be angry
at General Motors for burning up
all the Mack buses and all the green striped
trolleys, and at the concrete lobby
for selling motels and mobility to
a clubby bunch of Babbitt individualists.
At Girard, where you snake off
into your favorite Philadelphia,
your Firestones skidding over the glassy
tracks laid down between granite
cobbles by a gang of fresh Sicilians
a hundred years ago, you'll remember
that Mumford was right about
the car being the death of cities.

And before you hit the plywood district,
before the bombed-out Schmidts
Brewery and the old Jewish neighborhoods
now lined with flag and gun shop Joes and
crackhouses and that one skinny whore with
a mouthful of rotten teeth, you remember
that you want to love this city.

You grind your teeth a little bit, maybe rip
a little flesh from your lower lip, and just
a block beyond Front you left onto Second
and head for Vine, for art at the Painted Bride.
If you're honest this is where you begin to cry.
Old City, they call it. If only it were Prague.
And you've questioned it a hundred times
and you keep on hearing the answers always
making as much sense as before: what the hell
happened here? What coal-freight derailed
through this neighborhood? And tell me,
How long's it been gone? And whose fire's
comin' next time, anyway? You're crazy.
It's then you curse: the no parking, the parking
from eight a.m. to six-thirty p.m. Monday or
Wednesday or Thursday except, and Saturday
and Sunday and no goddam parking anytime
because it's a sacred tow away zone from here
to Detroit, home of holy blasphemy and liars.

You want to remember, you, before you
escaped to the empty suburbs, what it was like.
You want to love your neighbor, the way
your mother loved Mrs. Fritz two doors down
at 1516, who spent untold hours in dark
lonely humidity in a rowhouse brickie in
Northern Liberties because she didn't have a
few lousy bucks for a caved-in front porch.

You think of her, and your mother, wheezing
from all that airborne fuzz molded into a fine
Stetson fitted for a Dilworth or a Cecil B. Moore.
She did it for you, loved her neighbors even
if they were German Marxists, and you know it,
and you wonder how in the hell you're going
to face her when she's frozen beneath Our Holy
Savior behind Bob's Diner on Ridge Avenue.
You, living in Pheasant Run, in Vinyl City,
cooped in the big beige, driving the big beige.

You try as hard as you can, you keep it before you
and stare into it like that bug-eyed Rizzo poster
in Fat Edna's on Manayunk and Vassar and you
get up to piss and look into that mirror—
you remember: you want to love this city.
And you do and you mean it and you cry for it and
you swear it. You do. For the love of your friends
still living here in the impossible goddamn it you do.

BRICK

It's your wide face,
public; your east

always a hopeful blue,
your west an orange

refractory dream.
Your granular crisp

warm to touch
in glancing sun. It's

how ferociously
you abrade the cheek,

defy all question,
all mercy.

It's how you pluck
and pinch my hair

when I roll around
on you.

Wingless bird,
who could not

but fall for you.
Heft perfect

for walk, for run,
for scorn, for revolution.

Then so right, so flat
for the sweeping—

the scupped joints
hollowed just so.

I envy
your absorbent

gravity,
your specific heat,

your shield thick
against the burning.

I envy
your dry chemistry,

the pasty green
cellar ooze,

your crystalline,
spalling lime.

Just wait, just once
I'm going to chew

your impossible porosity.
Spit your dust.

Press your red
to mine.

IV

WHEN HOME, IN THE COCOON ...

for Jane Carroll and David Nagel

When home, in the cocoon of my flanneled sheets,
it was the long and continuous sounds that I liked the most:
those early heavy freights chugging around the river
on to the rolling mills and coal yards at Fairless, then back
to Camden and to soup and to stations and old RCAs.
Monday mornings were the best. In rain the sweetest.
Home was a Christmas, the gift of sleep all red and wrapped
and so full of easy question.

At sea, it was the outrageous whining and whining
and whining of the electric steam turbine so loud
and beautifully obliterating you could only scream back,
or sleep inside yourself like a cupped stone in a hand.
It was that extremity of noise, the narcotic of wave blue
after wave blue and the rocking steadiness that I loved.

Now, walled here in the city of brick and light,
in the dawn-orange cochlea of the bedroom,
it is Susan in the shower that is my luscious rain
of drug and sleep. Comes the electric hair dryer,
body long and smooth and beautifully blond,
strawberry; comes a little Egyptian musk
and goes a sandwich tucked a kiss good-bye Monday
Wednesday Friday, Saturday, and then, then
precious Sunday, at five-fifteen a.m.—it's them:

those damn bakery trucks on Krams Avenue.
Those damn back-up beepers shriving my soul.
Then it's that bread you hate the most—
when you wonder what crazy would eat such stuff,
when you wonder why in the hell you're living here,
when you wonder why in the hell you're so city poor,
when you wonder why in the hell your old man
married another mucked-up emotional catastrophe,
when you wonder why in the hell you love Smith's cat
more than you love your own steelworking brother,
why in the hell there has to be a god at five-fifteen a.m.
Who cares? For this this this; that that that. A tiny bit of sound.
You try breathing again. You try crawling again,
to wiggle your fins. It's then the wool is never thick enough
and you couldn't drown for all the world.

PHOTOSONATA

Of your skin, shops, and streets,
        I sneaked and looted everything
                for a keepsake joy and treasure—

for a picture-book of little songs
        that came first as a latent crystal halide
                on a tongue of cellulose film calling

for light—
        a coil of secrets that spoke
                of my love for citrics and sulphates,

for black-and-white, for touch, face, eye, see—
        O you city
                O happy sickly nobody everybody you.

CAPTIONS

I – EASTERN PENNSYLVANIA

2	Rolling mills and coke works, Bethlehem Steel, Bethlehem, 1990
22	View west from Minsi Trail Bridge, Bethlehem Steel, Bethlehem, 1990
25	Auto mechanics (former industrial workers), Northampton County, 1993
27	Coal miners, Windber, 1990
29	Former industrial worker and son, Northampton County, 1990
31	Office secretaries (former industrial workers), Ctr. Square, Easton, 1990
32	"B&J Knitters," Pottsville, 1992
33	Single-needle garment worker, Martin Shirt Co., Shenandoah, 1992
35	Former garment worker, Easton, 1991
37	Papermill worker and daughter, Northampton County, 1990
39	Former steelworkers, Bethlehem, 1998
41	Recent arrivals, North 7th Street, Allentown, 1996
42	Youth, North 7th Street, Allentown, 1996
43	Recent arrivals, North 7th Street, Allentown, 1996

II – CENTRAL, WESTERN, AND EASTERN PENNSYLVANIA

46	Window and crane hoist, The Bethlehem Corporation, Bethlehem, 1989
47	Auto mechanics (former industrial workers), Northampton County, 1993
49	Industrial crane operator, Northampton County, 1990
50	High tensions, Bethlehem Steel, Bethlehem, 1990
51	Former steelworker, Northampton County, 1991
53	Former foundry workers, Center Square, Easton, 1990
55	Industrial welder and daughter, Northampton County, 1990
56	Mechanic and Perry Streets, Bethlehem, 1998

PARTICIPANTS

THE AUTHOR WISHES TO THANK THE FOLLOWING:

William Jay Barrett, Philadelphia

Joyce J. Baskins, Philadelphia

Ben, southside Bethlehem

Frank Bond, Philadelphia

Walkeen Brown, Philadelphia

Lyle Burns, Northampton County

Jane Carroll and David Nagel, Philadelphia

John Charnego, Windber

William Christensen, Northampton County

Russell L. Christian, Northampton County

Robert L. Claus, Northampton County

Louis Cordero, Jr., Philadelphia

Maurice Davis, Philadelphia

Percy A. Davis, Westmoreland County

Lenora Decker, Northampton County

Lisa N. Decker, Northampton County

Robert Delker, Sr., Northampton County

Robert S. Delker, Northampton County

Thomas G. Demko, Burgettstown

Cheryl Eck, Northampton County

Kenneth D. Eck, Northampton County

Michael J. Garrity, Northampton County

Tracy T. Glisson, Berks County

Anthony Gonzales, Philadelphia

George Hockman, Sr., Northampton County

George Hockman, Jr., Northampton County

Marcus Ingram, Philadelphia

Rose Liberti, Northampton County

Enrique Marrero, Northampton County

Marie M. Martin, Northampton County

Mary Ann Martin, Northampton County

Delos Miller, Windber

Scott Molnar, Northampton County

Tara Molnar, Northampton County

Russell E. Moser, Northampton County

Chris Myers, Northampton County

Isaiah Nathaniel, Philadelphia

Lee Nathaniel, Philadelphia

John E. Paolini, Northampton County

John J. Paolini, Northampton County

Chance Pascual, Northampton County

Charles K. Peter, Bucks County

Laron Ragland, Philadelphia

John Richardson, Pottsville

Lester Rittenhouse, Northampton County

Anthony Rodriguez, Allentown

Claudio Rosaria, Lehigh County

Marino Rosario, Lehigh County

Louis Roselli, Philadelphia

Sally Ross, Northampton County

Helen E. Scholtis, Schuylkill County

Charles Smith, Northampton County

David W. Smith, Northampton County

James E. Smith, Philadelphia

Michael Standard, Westmoreland County

Ernest L. Stires, Warren County, NJ

William Strahle, Northampton County

Charles Swint, Northampton County

Swan Vacula, Lehigh County

Javier Vasquez, Philadelphia

Martin Washko, Windber

J. Weasner, Northampton County

Ivan Witherspoon, Philadelphia

Clyde Zuccal, Northampton County

George T. Ridout, Sr., Philadelphia

SELECTED EXHIBITS

FACES FROM AN AMERICAN DREAM

Harvard University, Carpenter Center, Visual and Environmental Studies

Dartmouth College, Hopkins Center for the Arts, Hanover, NH

Queen's University, Dept. of Languages, Arts, Film Studies, Belfast, Northern Ireland

New York University, Leonard N. Stern School of Business, Management Edu. Ctr.

Fordham University, Lincoln Center Campus, New York, NY

Cornell University, School of Industrial and Labor Relations, Ithaca, NY

Provincetown Fine Arts Work Center, Provincetown, MA (with poet Gerald Stern)

Wellfleet Public Library, Wellfleet, MA (with literary program)

United States Senate, Russell Rotunda, Washington, DC

United States Department of Labor, Washington, DC

George Meany Memorial Archives, Washington, DC

University of the Arts, Gallery 1401, Philadelphia, PA

Arcadia University, Landman Library, Philadelphia, PA (with literary program)

The Painted Bride Art Center, Philadelphia, PA

College of Textiles and Science, Philadelphia, PA (with literary program)

Roosevelt University, School of Social Justice, Chicago, IL

College of DuPage, McAninch Arts Center, Chicago, IL (with literary program)

Southern Illinois University, University Museum, Carbondale, IL

Michigan State University, College of Law, East Lansing, MI

Marlboro College, Drury Art Gallery, Marlboro, VT (with poet F. D. Reeve)

New England College, Henniker, NH (with literary program)

Seton Hall University, Walsh Library, South Orange, NJ (with literary program)

Lafayette College, Williams Center for the Arts, Easton, PA

Lafayette College, *Martin Desht: Photographs, 1987-1997* (with poet Sekou Sundiata)

Muhlenberg College, Pennsylvania Historical Assn. Convention, Allentown, PA

Pennsylvania State University, Pattee Libraries, State College, PA

Santa Fe Community College, Santa Fe, NM

Santa Fe Public Library, Santa Fe, NM

Unitarian Universalist Congregation Gallery, Santa Fe, NM

Albright College, Reading, PA (with photographer Joseph Elliot)

The American Labor Museum, Paterson, NJ

Indiana University of Pennsylvania, Kipp Gallery of Art, Indiana, PA

DeSales University, Center Valley, PA (with poet Ross Gay)

Northampton Community College, Bethlehem, PA (with poet Len Roberts)

Quadrant Books, Easton, PA (with poet Gerald Stern)

Connexions Gallery, Easton, PA (GUN FREE ZONE)

North Dakota Art Association, Minot, ND (online)

University of Scranton Art Gallery, Scranton, PA (with literary program)

Youngstown State University, Museum of Industry and Labor, Youngstown, OH

A CERTAIN PEACE: ACCEPTANCE AND DEFIANCE IN NORTHERN IRELAND

School for Advanced Research, Santa Fe, NM

Wellfleet Public Library, Wellfleet, MA

Lafayette College, Easton, PA (with lecture and literary program)

Santa Fe Public Library, Santa Fe, NM

DeSales University, Center Valley, PA (with poet Ross Gay)

GROUP EXHIBITS:

ERASE HATE: CREATE A NEW WORLD, AN EXHIBIT ON RACISM IN AMERICA
The Puffin Foundation, Ltd., The Cultural Center, New York, NY, 1999-2000

KRISTALLNACHT REFLECTIONS: 1938-1998
Holocaust Museum & Resource Center, Everhart Museum, Scranton, PA, 1998

IMAGE–TEXT RELATIONSHIPS

TEXTS THAT ACCOMPANY PHOTOGRAPHS always serve an author's purpose and usually operate in one or more roles. *Extra-photographic* texts can appropriate visual clues from the image, ignore or attempt to remain neutral to visual clues, take advantage of ambiguous clues to suggest a particular interpretation, or wholly invent "clues" in an attempt to coerce a viewpoint or an interpretation. *Intra-photographic* texts can appear as part of the image or be the entire image itself and can operate similarly. The relationships outlined below are not conclusive.

1. Extra-photographic text (e.g., an external caption) defines image.

    A. Text supports image by:

        1. Reducing image to an illustration of text.

    B. Text subverts image by:

        1. Limiting interpretation of image.

        2. Indicating or betraying authorial use or intention.

2. Image subverts extra-photographic text.

    A. Text subverted if seen as:

        1. Neutral, arbitrary, or superfluous appendage.

        2. Understatement.

        3. Ambiguous.

        4. Presenting linguistic or idiomatic confusion.

        5. Foreign language.

    B. Viewer interprets visual clues non-supportive of text.

    (Image permits multiple narratives.)

3. Extra-photographic text, image, and viewer collaborate to agree on meaning.

4. Extra-photographic text, image, and viewer collaborate to disagree on meaning.

   A. Authorial use or intent in conflict with viewer's internalized interpretation.

      1. Cultural information influences viewer's internalized interpretation.

         a. Viewer re-imagines image's use and meaning.
         b. Viewer re-imagines text's use and meaning.

5. Intra-photographic text (text within a photograph) alone or combined with extra-photographic text.

   A. Combined intra-photographic text as:

      1. Supporting extra-photographic text.
      2. Subverting extra-photographic text.
      3. Defining image.
      4. Defining intention and use.

   B. Intra-photographic text alone as:

      1. Defining image.
      2. Defining intention and use.

———

Three lively discussions on documentary work are Susan Sontag's *On Photography*, William Stott's *Documentary Expression and Thirties America*, and Alan Trachtenberg's *Reading American Photographs: Images as History–Mathew Brady to Walker Evans*. Each is very accessible and a treasure of reward.

Other work by Martin J. Desht:
Growing Up in an Industrial Age
Factory Work I (catalogue)
Factory Work II (catalogue)

Documentary exhibits:
GUN FREE ZONE
FACES FROM AN AMERICAN DREAM
A CERTAIN PEACE: ACCEPTANCE AND DEFIANCE IN NORTHERN IRELAND

"Because You Want To Love" and "When home, in the cocoon ..." first appeared in *New Letters*. "Crane Gang" first appeared as a poem in *Entelechy International*. Photo-essays with prose or poems have appeared in *Pennsylvania History*, *Living Forge* (with poetry by Philip Levine), *The International Journal of Regional and Local Studies* (UK), *Alembic Review*, *Nightsun*, *Review of Arts, Literature, Philosophy*, *HEART* (Human Equity Through ART), *Newsletter of the Center for Working-class Studies* at Youngstown State University, *Two Rivers Review*, *Labor's Heritage*, *Kiosk Magazine*, *Exquisite Corpse* (Andrei Codrescu, ed.).

Publisher's Cataloging-in-Publication data

Desht, Martin J. (Martin Joseph), 1949-
   Photosonata / Martin J. Desht ; foreword by Gerald Stern.
   p. cm.
   ISBN 978-0-692-35937-2

1. Documentary photography—United States. 2. Working class—Pennsylvania—Pictorial works. 3. Philadelphia (Pa.)—Pictorial works. 4. Working class—Pennsylvania—Philadelphia—Pictorial works. 5. Philadelphia (Pa.)—Social conditions—20th century—Pictorial works. 6. Poetry. 7. Photography, artistic. I. Stern, Gerald, 1925-. II. Title.

HD8083.P43 D47 2015
305.562—dc23   2014922883

First Edition 2015
Library of Congress Control Number: 2014922883
FINE GRAIN BOOKS - SANTA FE / Email: FGB2014@post.com
Book design: Heumiller-Desht / Cover design © Heumiller-Desht 2015
Printed and bound in the United States of America